THE ACOUSTIC ROCK GUITAR BOOK

Master the Acoustic Techniques, Riffs & Songwriting of Rock's Greatest Guitarists

STUART RYAN

FUNDAMENTAL CHANGES

The Acoustic Rock Guitar Book

Master the Acoustic Techniques, Riffs & Songwriting of Rock's Greatest Guitarists

ISBN: 978-1-78933-466-1

Published by **www.fundamental-changes.com**

Copyright © 2025 Stuart Ryan

Edited by Joseph Alexander

www.fundamental-changes.com

For over 350 free guitar lessons with videos check out:

www.fundamental-changes.com

Join our free Facebook Community of Cool Musicians

www.facebook.com/groups/fundamentalguitar

Tag us for a share on Instagram: FundamentalChanges

Cover Image Copyright: Shutterstock

Contents

Introduction

It's easy to think of the acoustic guitar as a supporting instrument in rock, but in reality, it can often define a song. Imagine The Eagles' *Hotel California* without its iconic twelve-string picking pattern or *Angie* without Keith Richards' plaintive acoustic riff. The same applies to classic tunes by The Beatles, Led Zeppelin, Kansas, Sheryl Crow, and countless others. All of these artists have shaped their sound and created legendary tracks with the acoustic guitar.

The beauty of the acoustic guitar lies in its versatility. It can provide a rich, supportive foundation, but in the right hands, its tone can take centre stage. In this book, you will learn how well-voiced chords bring depth and personality, how fingerpicking adds detail and energy, and how great players craft intros, riffs, and rhythm parts using just one acoustic guitar.

Like electric guitars, different acoustic models have distinct tonal qualities, with certain brands excelling in specific areas. The defining sounds of 1960s' rock were shaped by Martin D-28s, D-18s, and Gibson J-45s and J-200s. As acoustic tones evolved, the bright shimmer of Ovations in the 1970s gave way to the refined clarity of Taylor 414s from the 1990s onwards. Some guitars are built for bold, open-chord strumming, while others shine in fingerpicked arrangements. If there were one perfect guitar for this journey, it might be the Martin D-28. However, an old Gibson J-45 or a Martin 000-18 would be just as inspiring.

Let's get started.

Get the Audio

The audio files for this book are available to download for free from **www.fundamental-changes.com.** The link is in the top right-hand corner. Click on the "Guitar" link then simply select this book title from the drop-down menu and follow the instructions to get the audio.

We recommend that you download the files directly to your computer, not to your tablet, and extract them there before that adds them to your media library.

For over 350 free guitar lessons with videos check out:

www.fundamental-changes.com

Join our free Facebook Community of Cool Musicians

www.facebook.com/groups/fundamentalguitar

Tag us for a share on Instagram: **FundamentalChanges**

Chapter One – Colour Chords

The open position accounts for a huge part of acoustic rock's style. Chords played here take advantage of the guitar's natural resonance, adding brightness that complements the ring of cymbals and hi-hat. Some artists strum open chords as a simple rhythmic device, while others add colour to make their parts distinctive and memorable. Think of the section just before the solo of *Stairway to Heaven* where Jimmy Page creates a simple yet unforgettable riff around an open D Major chord.

Colour in chords comes from going beyond their basic structure. A C Major chord is built from a root (C), 3rd (E), and 5th (G), but adding a major 7th (B), a 9th (D), the tension of the 11th (F), or even the #11 (F#), introduces new character. These embellishments are often located just a fret or two away from the basic chord and can normally be accessed by simply moving a finger.

The open D Major shape is one of the most embellished chords in acoustic rock. Remove the second finger from the 2nd fret of the E string and add the open E to play a Dsus2 chord. Place the fourth finger on the 3rd fret and you create a Dsus4 chord. Both have an ambiguous sound that songwriters love.

Example 1a

This 1970s piano-rock-style progression is built around the D Major shape. The descent on the B string takes you on a journey from D Major to DMaj7 and then to D7, which strongly pulls to the IV chord, GMaj7. All very "Elton John".

Example 1b

Here's the same idea on a G Major chord and again you will hear the pull from G7 to the IV chord, C Major. Start with the third finger on the low E string and the fourth on the high E. Then, use the second and first fingers to play the descending melody notes.

Example 1c

You can also move the inner voices of a G Major to great effect and here's one way to do that on the G string. Place the second finger on low E string and the third on the high E. Now use the first and fourth fingers on the G string in turn.

Example 1d

Songwriters often move from a straight major to a major 7th chord, then add colour by introducing a 9th. In this example, that movement takes place on the second string, with the gorgeous and ubiquitous Cadd9 appearing in bar two.

Example 1e

The previous examples have not required too much finger wrangling, but moving around an open E Major can be challenging. Try using your third finger on the A string, fourth on the D string, and second on the G string. To get to EMaj7, replace the fourth with the first on the D string, while keeping the other fingers in place.

Example 1f

Sometimes we simply need to modify our finger positions, and we can look at that now with an open A Major. Use your 2nd finger on the D string, third on the G string, and fourth on the B string. To play the AMaj7, replace your third finger with the first at the 1st fret.

Example 1g

Adding colour to chords can create interesting tensions, and that is the case with the next example. This sound is not as common, but the tension creates a dramatic quality sometimes found in 1970s rock. The A Major b6 chord has a dark sound, and you would usually move on from it quickly.

Example 1h

Playing moving basslines and broken chords can give a great approximation of a piano's voicings. Think of Paul McCartney's *Yesterday* when playing this next example where the ascending bassline from an open-position G Major chord adds character. Try strumming with the pick or articulating each string with the fingers.

Example 1i

Now the bass notes descend within the chords in a 1990s-style Noel Gallagher approach. The third and fourth fingers stay on the B and high E strings, while everything else moves around them. Your second finger starts on the 3rd fret and moves to the 2nd in bar two. This creates a smooth transition from G to the D by moving the bass note to the 3rd of D (F#).

Example 1j

Reverse the previous example and the same fingerings can be used. This time you play a full G Major chord in bar two while adding the major 3rd (B) on the 2nd fret before landing on the ii chord, Am7.

Example 1k

Mr Bond, I presume? In the '70s, artists began exploring dramatic chord progressions where the colour came from unpredictable movements rather than shifting notes within a chord shape. This sequence creates unstable movement through three keys: E, C, and A. Notice how the E at the 2nd fret of the D string and the open E link the chords.

Example 1l

This next example requires a specific fingering owing to the descending bassline.

- Play the D Major chord with your first finger barring the G, B, and high E strings

- Place your second finger at the 3rd fret of the B string

- Next, use your third or fourth finger for the bass note on the A string

- Finally, widen the barre to cover everything from the A string down to fret the B Minor chord

11

Example 1m

This moving bassline requires some forward planning and movement with barre chords.

- Play the A Major with a first finger barre across the 2nd fret of the D, G, and B strings

- Keep the barre in place, then use your third or fourth finger to play the bass note at the 4th fret

- For the F# Minor seven, extend the barre so it covers everything from the low E string down

Example 1n

Some artists find chord movements they love and use them repeatedly in their songwriting. Noel Gallagher often takes this approach with common tones (notes that stay in place as the chords change). On beat 2 of bar one, you might expect to hear an A Minor chord, but keeping the top half of the G Major in place while changing the bass note to an A creates a colourful A7sus4.

Example 1o

Chord inversions can be used to create smooth movements between chords. In this example, the G Major is played in first inversion (the 3rd of the chord, B, is played in the bass). This creates a smooth bassline that ascends from A to B to C. It is a simple yet effective alternative to jumping to a root position G Major shape.

Example 1p

Understanding how to add colour to your chords is one of the most effective ways to create interest and depth in your playing. By making subtle changes, such as adding suspended tones, altering bass notes, or introducing unexpected inversions, you can transform even the simplest progression into something rich and expressive.

As you move forward, keep experimenting with these ideas and listen for how different chord voicings affect the mood and movement of a song. The best acoustic guitarists use these techniques instinctively, and with practice, you will too.

In the next chapter, we will explore fingerpicking, which is one of the most versatile and expressive techniques on acoustic guitar. You will learn how to develop independence in your picking hand, create flowing arpeggios, and bring new textures to your playing.

Chapter Two – Fingerpicking

Fingerpicking is an essential part of the acoustic rock guitar toolkit. For some players, it is simply a method of accompaniment, using basic strumming and arpeggios. For others, like Jimmy Page, it becomes a detailed and complex technique that sounds more like a solo guitar piece. Some players take a folk or quasi-classical approach, while others, like Keith Richards, bring a raw, blues-influenced aggression to their fingerpicking. Paul McCartney took an entirely different route, developing a style based around the ukulele, using only his thumb and index finger on his picking hand

This chapter introduces fingerpicking techniques in preparation for the examples later in the book. There are several approaches to fingerstyle, but it is best to begin with the folk/classical method. This means using the thumb to play the low E, A, and D strings while the index, middle, and ring fingers pluck the G, B, and high E strings, respectively. These patterns will vary depending on the player or context, but this approach provides a solid foundation for many picking parts.

This pattern uses that approach, with the thumb playing the A string while the index, middle, and ring fingers pluck the G, B, and E strings.

Keep your timing solid by counting "1 & 2 & 3 & 4 &" for each pluck.

Example 2a

Alternating bass notes create a more dynamic, musical texture in your playing. In this example, the thumb moves between notes on the A and D strings while the other fingers maintain the previous pattern. Developing independence in the thumb can be challenging at first, so take it slowly.

Example 2b

Cmaj

Many fingerpicking patterns require string skipping in cross-picking movements. If you are new to this technique, it may feel unnatural at first. Though the same fingers play the same strings, the pattern has changed, so approach this carefully and focus on achieving even timing.

Example 2c

Cmaj

Now the thumb plays an alternating bassline from the A to the D string while the other fingers follow the pattern from the previous example. It may look simple, but at first this can feel like information overload.

Example 2d

Cmaj

Altering picking patterns can help develop fluidity in your playing. One way to approach this is by using the thumb for the A and D strings while the index and middle fingers pluck the G and B strings. However, you could use the thumb for the A string, then the middle finger for the G string, followed by the index plucking the D string and the ring striking the B string.

Example 2e

Cmaj

Many patterns are based on plucking *rolls* that move either up or down the strings. Reverse rolls like this one require practice at first. Be mindful of accurately timing the upward roll using the ring, middle, and index fingers on the E, B, and G strings.

Example 2f

Eventually, your picking-hand fingers should operate on autopilot so you can focus on your fretting hand. I like to think of fretting fingers as my "content" and picking fingers as my "voice". This pattern introduces movement on the E, A, and D strings, so aim to shift your focus onto the fretting hand while keeping the picking hand steady.

Example 2g

The next example is similar to how a pianist's left and right hands interact. It follows a simple bass note and chord pattern, but as always, there are multiple ways to approach it. The thumb plays the bass note on the A string while the fingers pluck the G, B, and E strings together. Some players, such as Mark Knopfler, might strike these strings with the nail of the index finger or with the nails of the index, middle, and ring fingers together to create a completely different tone.

Example 2h

Try both picking approaches in this next example, which introduces a moving bassline beneath a static chord. This combination is a common songwriting tool in acoustic rock.

Example 2i

Now it is time to explore more complex rhythms. Here, the picking-hand fingering remains the same, but the rhythm now follows a "1 & a 2 & a 3 & a 4 & a" count. This creates quicker movements between the middle finger fretting the B string and the index striking the G string.

Example 2j

This example is inspired by Paul McCartney's classical-style approach in *Blackbird*. The picking-hand fingering remains unchanged, but now you are playing two notes simultaneously in 10ths (a 3rd plus an octave). This pattern works well as a solo guitar intro or as accompaniment to a vocal melody.

Example 2k

Reverse rolls with moving bass notes require careful concentration. Keep your focus on accuracy in the picking hand. Before attempting this example, ensure that your fretting hand is comfortable with the required shapes. Though it may look complex, you are ultimately playing four chord shapes and picking notes from within each one.

Example 2l

Broken chords with alternating basslines can appear difficult, but this example is built around an open C Major chord. The only movement occurs in the bassline, where the ring finger shifts from the A to the D string, and then to the E string. Listen to Paul Simon's *The Boxer* for a great example of this technique in action.

Example 2m

The next example follows a similar concept, except the picking-hand fingers now focus on the G, B, and high E strings. Assign the index finger to the G string, the middle to the B string, and the ring to the high E string.

Example 2n

Once you are familiar with these patterns, you can easily transpose them to different chords or make subtle variations. Here is a broken A Major chord with an alternating bassline. Some basslines move between the A string and the low E string, while others shift between the A and D strings. The choice generally depends on whether the root/octave or root/5th relationship best suits the chord shape.

Example 2o

For some chords, alternating bass patterns may involve string skipping. In this G Major idea, you create a root/5th bassline, moving from the 3rd fret of the low E string to the open D.

Example 2p

Now the same idea is applied to an open E Major chord, with the bassline alternating between the root and octave. One of great aspects of fingerpicking is that once your picking hand is comfortable with a pattern, you can easily change what your fretting hand plays to create new ideas or move to different keys.

Example 2q

Here is a common alternating bass pattern on a D Major chord. Some players modify their picking hand fingering so that the thumb plays the A, D, and G strings while the first finger plucks the B string, and the middle finger strikes the high E. This variation might feel smoother than the patterns covered so far.

Example 2r

Drop D tuning became an acoustic staple from the mid-1960s onwards. A great example is John Lennon's playing on *Dear Prudence*, where the two D strings form the alternating bassline while melodies and chords are played over the top. There is a tricky syncopation in bar two, so listen to the audio to ensure you are locking into the groove.

Example 2s

Not every note needs to be picked, and hammer-ons and pull-offs are often used to lighten the workload for the picking hand. In bar two, a syncopated rhythm combines with a G string hammer-on to create another challenging timing exercise.

Example 2t

This example focuses on syncopation. The alternating bassline follows a steady "1 & 2 & 3 & 4 &" count, while the melody notes fall around the beats. Many artists internalise these patterns and reuse them across different chord shapes.

Example 2u

This final example borrows rhythmic ideas from John Lennon's *Dear Prudence*, using triads along the upper strings. Get the chord shapes in place first, as your focus should be on the picking hand rather than the fretting hand. Assigning the index, middle, and ring fingers to their correct strings eliminates any guesswork in the picking hand.

Example 2v

Fingerpicking is one of the most expressive techniques available to an acoustic guitarist. Whether used for delicate ballads, intricate folk-style arrangements, or rhythmically complex rock accompaniment, it brings depth and colour to your playing. By now, you should feel comfortable with alternating basslines, syncopated melodies, and the interplay between fretted and open strings.

To build on these ideas, try applying fingerpicking to chord progressions you already know. Experiment with different tempos and dynamics, and study players like Mark Knopfler, James Taylor, and Nick Drake to see how they bring fingerstyle techniques into their songwriting.

In the next chapter, we explore the pioneers of acoustic rock from the 1960s. You will study how Keith Richards wove blues and folk influences into The Rolling Stones' music, how Pete Townshend's percussive acoustic style helped define The Who, and how The Beatles crafted timeless acoustic parts.

Chapter Three – Artists of the 1960s

Throughout the 1930s, '40s, and '50s, the acoustic guitar found its home in bluegrass, country and western, and folk music. Country stars like Hank Williams and Johnny Cash strummed Martin and Gibson acoustics, while electric guitars handled the more intricate lead parts. In fact, the new opportunity to amplify electric guitars pushed acoustics into the background in many ways.

In the 1960s, however, a new generation of songwriters emerged, for whom the acoustic guitar was just as much a creative tool as the electric. Artists like Ray Davies, Keith Richards, John Lennon, and Paul McCartney developed distinctive voices on acoustic guitar. No longer just a background instrument for strumming, the acoustic guitar became the centrepiece of many songs. Tracks like *Yesterday*, *Norwegian Wood*, and The Kinks' *Lola* showcase an intimate connection between songwriter and instrument.

In this chapter, you will explore how each artist brought a unique approach to acoustic guitar, from Keith Richards' Delta blues influences to Paul McCartney's Bach-inspired passages.

Let's jump in.

Keith Richards

While many of The Rolling Stones' biggest tracks were built around fuzz-laden electric riffs, such as *Satisfaction*, or R&B-inspired grooves like *Brown Sugar*, there are many that feature intimate acoustic guitar parts in both standard and altered tunings. Keith Richards is a great player to study, as his acoustic work blends rhythm and lead, often within the same bar.

Deeply rooted in the blues, his playing weaves around the vocal line without overpowering it. The way he and Mick Jagger interact, particularly on stripped-back songs like *Wild Horses* and *Angie*, shows just how important his acoustic guitar parts are in shaping the Stones' sound.

On *Country Honk*, Keith moves effortlessly between chords and licks. The first four bars use the colour chord approach you studied in Chapter One to make a simple G Major to C Major progression more expressive. The bluesy lick in bar five completes the feel, making for a dynamic accompaniment part.

Example 3a

Gmaj   Dsus2   Dadd9/F♯   G5

Keith often brings electric guitar rhythm ideas into his acoustic playing. In this example, you are using *Brown Sugar*-style major triads on the D, G, and B strings, with the open A string acting as a pedal tone. The A string belongs in both the A Major and D Major chords, but listen to how the G Major creates a cool, unexpected colour.

Example 3b

Amaj   Dmaj/A Amaj   Dmaj/A   Gmaj/A Dmaj/A

Some of Richards' acoustic parts are incredibly detailed. This approach works beautifully on slower tracks like *Angie*, where there is so much space to fill. In bar two, you will find a rich "colour chords on steroids" sound, built around G Major chord variations. Work through this slowly as there's a lot going on.

Example 3c

Here, begin by learning the bassline, and listen carefully the audio. Apart from on beat 1, the open D string forms a constant bassline played both on and off the beat. The top notes are syncopated, similar to the patterns you studied at the end of Chapter Two.

Example 3d

This is another great example of how Keith Richards weaves complex ideas into simple chord progressions. The feel is bluesy, played in a 12/8 time signature, so count "1 & a 2 & a 3 & a 4 & a" to get into the triplet groove. I recommend learning this chord by chord, as there is a lot of detail to absorb.

Example 3e

Pete Townshend

One of rock's first true showmen, Pete Townshend's explosive power chords were the driving force behind The Who. But acoustic guitars played just as vital a role in their sound. Tracks like *Pinball Wizard* and *Behind Blue Eyes* feature classic acoustic riffs that have become essential learning for any rock guitarist.

Townshend often played a Gibson J-200, a guitar that suited his powerful strumming style. His aggressive attack demands an instrument that can handle a heavy hand, making the J-200 a perfect choice.

This simple picked part is all about adding colour to basic chords. The C Major chord is expanded with the addition of a D (the 9th), while in bar three, the A Major chord swaps the 3rd (C#) for the 9th (B), to create a suspended tension that's typical of Townshend's approach.

Example 3f

The FMaj7 in bar three is a classic 1960s chord voicing. To play it, hook your thumb over the neck to play the 1st fret of the low E string, leaving your other fingers free to shape the rest of the chord. Make sure you get the "1 2& 3 4 5 6" count correct.

Example 3g

Much of Townshend's acoustic rhythm playing has a choppy, percussive feel. His speed and fluency require a completely relaxed strumming hand. This example includes a suggested strumming pattern to help develop the right feel.

Example 3h

Moving major and minor triads up and down the treble strings against a pedal tone is one of Townshend's most distinctive techniques and you can hear this approach in tracks like *Substitute*. A suggested strumming pattern is included here.

Example 3i

Townshend often contrasts his wild rhythm style with gentle, folk-inspired fingerpicking, as heard on tracks like *I'm One*. This example is built around G Major and C Major chord shapes and uses embellishments similar to those you worked on in Chapter Two. Start with the alternating bass, then add the melody on top.

Example 3j

Ray Davies

The Kinks drew inspiration from a wide range of sources, including the rock 'n' roll of Chuck Berry and Eddie Cochran, and the blues of John Lee Hooker. Their acoustic approach was shaped by British skiffle, music hall, and traditional folk. Like Townshend, Davies was a master of driving rhythms, interesting chord progressions, and colourful voicings.

This rhythm part reflects Davies' early influences, blending blues and rock 'n' roll. The Chuck Berry influence is clear, but slowing the tempo and playing it on acoustic gives it a different feel.

Example 3k

Ray Davies frequently used driving 1/16th-note rhythms in his playing. This style requires a loose, relaxed strumming hand. When strumming groups of 1/16th-note chords, you'd typically alternate downstrokes and upstrokes, but the chord hammer-on at the start complicates this pattern. A suggested strumming guide is provided.

Example 3l

A9sus4 Amaj   G5   Dadd9/F#

```
T   0~  0-0-0-0-0-0~  0-0-0-0-0-0   3-3-3-3-3---3-3-0-0-0-0-0---0-0
A   0-2-2-2-2-2-2-0-2-2-2-2-2-0   3-3-3-3-3---3-3-3-3-3-3-3---3-3
    0-2-2-2-2-2-2-0-2-2-2-2-2-0   0-0-0-0-0---0-0-2-2-2-2-2---2-2
B   0-2-2-2-2-2-2-0-2-2-2-2-2-0   0-0-0-0-0---0-0-0-0-0-0-0---0-0
    0~  0-0-0-0-0-0~  0-0-0-0-0-0                 0-0-0-0-0---0-0
                                  3-3-3-3-3---3-3-2-2-2-2-2---2-2
```

∏   ∏ V ∏ V ∏   ∏ V ∏ V ∏   ∏ V ∏ V ∏   ∏ V ∏ V ∏ V ∏ V ∏ ∏ V

This example revisits the triad/pedal tone approach seen in Pete Townshend's playing. Listen to how much colour the triads take on when played against the open D string. Though the chord progression only consists of primary triads (D, G, and A Major), the pedal tone transforms their character.

Example 3m

Dmaj   Gmaj/B Dmaj   Amaj/D   Gmaj/B Dmaj

```
T   2---2-2-2-------3---2   5---5-5-5-------3---2
A   3---3-3-3-------3---3   5---5-5-5-------3---3
    2---2-2-2-----4-----2   6---6-6-6-----4-----2
B   0---0-0-0---0-------0   0---0-0-0---0-------0
```

Davies often incorporated a swing feel reminiscent of early music hall and skiffle. Listen to The Kinks' *Dandy* to hear how he applies swing to acoustic guitar. It is a tricky feel to master, so be sure to listen to the recording.

Example 3n

Many guitarists use acoustic guitars to play clean-sounding arpeggios using open-position chords, but here, Davies moves higher up the neck, picking triads on the top three strings. This is an effective way to create parts that stand out in a busy mix, where open chords can sometimes sound muddy. You can hear this technique on The Kinks' *Get Back in Line*.

Example 3o

The Beatles – John/Paul/George

The Beatles had three highly individual guitarists, each bringing a unique approach to acoustic playing. John Lennon and Paul McCartney were drawn together by their love of skiffle, but their shared influence developed into quite contrasting styles. Lennon was inspired in part by Donovan's alternating bassline fingerpicking, while McCartney embraced elements of ukulele technique by using just his thumb and index finger. George Harrison's acoustic style was deeply influenced by Django Reinhardt and Carl Perkins, though it arguably became more pronounced in his solo career, particularly on *All Things Must Pass*.

George Harrison

This first example has a strong piano-style separation between bass and treble with strummed chords before isolated E, A, and D strings for clarity. The Django Reinhardt influence is evident in the tense C#Dim7 chord in bar three. You could also view this as a rootless A7b9, acting as a secondary dominant to D7 moving to G Major.

Example 3p

Place a capo on the 7th fret for this *Here Comes the Sun*-style part. Simple strummed open chords take on a fresh tone in this register, and the melody within the chord in bar two is clearer than it would be in open position. Softer-sounding suspended chords round out the feel.

Example 3q

Capo fret 7

G5   Dsus4 Dmaj Dsus2   Csus2   Dsus2

John Lennon

Lennon learned alternating bassline picking from Donovan and used it on tracks like *Dear Prudence*. Tune down to Drop D and get comfortable with the chord shapes on the top strings first, so you can focus fully on the picking-hand pattern. The chords themselves are simple major and minor triads, but the alternating bassline adds colour and movement.

Example 3r

Dmaj   Amaj/D   Am9/D

G/D   D

A descending bassline within an alternate picking pattern creates another important '60s sound. Here, the bassline moves down the low E string while the D string remains open. Keeping the third finger anchored on the B string throughout makes for a smooth transition to the D Major chord in the final bar.

Example 3s

Paul McCartney

McCartney has an idiosyncratic picking style and here the thumb takes care of the E, A, and D strings, while the index finger picks or flicks downwards on the remaining strings (a common ukulele technique). However, you will probably find it easier to play this idea with a more conventional picking approach. This part is written around the 10th intervals famously used in *Blackbird*.

Example 3t

The final example in this chapter reflects one of McCartney's approaches on descending basslines, similar to those heard in *Yesterday*. For authenticity, try his ukulele-style picking, where the thumb plays the bass notes and the index finger flicks down to play the chords. If you prefer a more conventional approach, use the thumb for the bass notes and pluck the top strings with the index, middle, and ring fingers.

Example 3u

The 1960s laid the foundation for acoustic rock guitar, with artists pushing the instrument beyond its traditional role as a simple rhythm tool. From the bluesy swagger of Keith Richards to the driving power of Pete Townshend, and the melodic innovations of The Beatles, this era saw the acoustic guitar take centre stage in rock music.

To further develop your playing, try adapting their techniques into your own songwriting. Experiment with Pete Townshend-style triads against pedal tones, incorporate Keith Richards' bluesy embellishments, or apply John Lennon's fingerpicking to different chord progressions.

In the next chapter, we step into the '70s, where acoustic guitars became even more prominent. You will explore how artists like David Bowie, Jimmy Page, and Brian May expanded the possibilities of the instrument, introducing new tunings, intricate fingerpicking, and complex harmonies.

Chapter Four – Artists of the 1970s Part One

In the 1970s, rock became a genre in its own right, and acoustic guitars became easier to use live. Acoustic guitar pickups had existed in some form since the 1930s, but by the 1970s the technology had improved enough that acoustics could be amplified more easily and taken on the road. Some artists still used microphones on stage, but the development of pickups made the process much easier and reduced feedback issues. As a result, acoustic guitars began to feature more prominently in rock, as their parts could be accurately reproduced on stage.

This chapter explores the artists who had just as much affinity for acoustics as they did electrics.

David Bowie

Everything Bowie did was unique, and this carried over into his approach to acoustic guitar. Sometimes, you are hearing his sideman Mick Ronson on acoustic, as is the case on *Ziggy Stardust*, so always bear in mind Ronson's creative genius too. It is not always easy to tell whether an artist or sideman played acoustic on certain tracks, but where possible, live footage can provide useful clues.

Acoustic guitars are superb instruments for creating tension and release. Playing simple chord shapes against open strings can produce a dark, clashing sound, as heard in the intro to *Starman*. This first example demonstrates how tension and resolution can go far beyond a typical IV–I chord movement.

Example 4a

Contrast the previous example with the softer colours of this chord progression, where sophisticated voicings are created through subtle movements within basic open chords. Placing a capo at the 5th fret brings out an even sweeter quality.

Example 4b

CAPO FRET 5

In Chapter One, you studied how moving notes within chords can introduce colour. This next example, inspired by Bowie's *My Death*, demonstrates that technique in action. The movement of notes on the B string once again creates tension and release.

Example 4c

This next example follows the same principle, this time with a descending movement on the B string within a D Major chord shape. The quickfire rhythms in bar three are typical of Bowie's strumming approach, so keep your wrist relaxed when playing the 1/16th notes.

Example 4d

This example builds on the previous ideas, but with the movement taking place on the A string. Notice how the rhythm in bar two closely resembles the previous example and highlights how artists can use rhythm as a feature just as much as harmony and melody.

Example 4e

Brian May

Acoustic guitars are not that prominent in Queen's catalogue, possibly because their typical piano and electric guitar arrangements did not leave much space for one. However, there are plenty of great acoustic moments in their music, from the ballad *Love of My Life* to the rockabilly-inspired swing of *Crazy Little Thing Called Love*. Brian May often played acoustic on stage, and while his electric style is widely discussed, his acoustic playing is less frequently examined.

The first example is inspired by *Crazy Little Thing Called Love* and features simple movement within a C Major chord shape. The original track is based around an open D Major shape, but the same principles apply here. The swing feel of the original is also present in this example.

Example 4f

Sometimes, all you need is simple chords and strumming. This example shows how that, combined with the power of a minor iv to major I resolution creates a classic songwriting technique. It's a simple idea, but strumming is often an effective technique.

Example 4g

Brian May is an excellent fingerpicker, and there is plenty of footage of him accompanying Freddie Mercury and Kerry Ellis on an acoustic guitar. In a situation like that, the guitarist is totally exposed, making your timing, tone, and dynamics crucial.

Example 4h

This next example introduces more detail, using broken chords and 6th intervals to outline the triads in bar three. You can play this fingerstyle, though some players may prefer hybrid picking. In this approach, the pick handles the lower strings, while the middle and ring fingers pluck the higher notes. The advantage of this approach is that you can seamlessly transition from broken chords to strumming with the pick.

Example 4i

Aside from his fingerpicking, May has excellent fretting-hand control and can move through chord shapes quickly. This next example focuses on rapid chord changes, an effect heard in Queen's *'39*.

Example 4j

David Gilmour

The acoustic guitar in Pink Floyd became gradually more prominent over the years, and often featured regularly in David Gilmour's solo work. In the Floyd's early years, the acoustic guitar was mainly used for support and to thicken their sound. Later, it would become the centrepiece of tracks like *Wish You Were Here*.

The fist Gilmour example adds colour to a chord sequence by exploring the flowing major, major 7th, and major 6th sounds often heard in Pink Floyd's music. Start with the second finger on the low E string and the fourth on the D string. In the next bar, the first finger takes care of the 2nd fret.

Example 4k

Gilmour often brought the dexterity of his electric playing to the acoustic guitar. This example incorporates hammer-ons and pull-offs around an Em chord, similar to the intro of *Wish You Were Here*.

Example 4l

This fingerpicking passage uses techniques covered in Chapter Two. First, get comfortable with the chord shapes, then introduce the picking-hand fingers. Fingerpicked arpeggios like this leave no room for error as any missed notes will stand out clearly.

Example 4m

Gilmour's blues influences are evident in his fingerstyle playing. Here, we play bluesy double-stops over a repeated pedal tone of the open D string. Listen to Pink Floyd's *Goodbye Blue Sky* to hear how this technique can be developed into a complete song part.

Example 4n

Dmaj Em7/D Amaj/D Dmaj Dmaj7 Gmaj/D

Rich chord voicings are another key feature of Gilmour's style. The Dadd4 chord in bar one is a favourite among acoustic players. It's easy to remember, as it is simply a C Major shape moved up two frets, but the open G string introduces a 4th for additional colour.

Example 4o

Dadd4

Am Gmaj Dadd4

Jimmy Page

Led Zeppelin's Jimmy Page is a multi-faceted guitarist. His playing draws from the blues influences of Hubert Sumlin, B.B. King, and Otis Rush, alongside the rockabilly phrasing of Scotty Moore and Cliff Gallup. But his acoustic work was shaped by the English folk traditions of Bert Jansch and the Middle Eastern sounds of Davey Graham. Page is one of the most technically advanced players in this book, and the following examples explore both standard and altered tunings, along with unusual time signatures like 7/8.

Page was highly attuned to the creative possibilities of the acoustic guitar and makes full use of its range. This example demonstrates the rich sound created by fretted notes against open strings. The E7sus2 at the end of bar one requires a stretch, so from low to high strings, use the first, second, third, and fourth fingers in sequence.

Example 4p

Simple altered tunings open up many creative possibilities. This example is in Double Drop D tuning, where both E strings are tuned down a whole step. The open strings do much of the harmonic work, supporting simple fretted chord shapes. Listen to *Going to California* to hear this technique in context.

Example 4q

From Double Drop D, it is a small step to DADGAD tuning by lowering the B string by a whole step. This tuning is associated with Page's folk-influenced side. The D11/C chord in bar four is challenging. It requires you to use the first finger to fret both the E and A strings at the 10th fret, while the third and second fingers handle the D and G strings.

Example 4r

Led Zeppelin often used odd time signatures. The challenge in this example is not in the fretting hand but the strumming hand, as it is played in 7/8 time. Listen carefully to the recording to internalise the feel.

Example 4s

Finally, this example introduces DGCGCD tuning, a staple of Page's acoustic work. It features in tracks like *The Rain Song* and reveals beautiful harmonic colours with simple parallel chord shapes.

Example 4t

Tuning - DGCGCD

We've explored a range of artists who shaped the acoustic rock sound of the 1970s, from the intricate folk stylings of Jimmy Page to the rhythmic drive of Pete Townshend and the songwriting genius of David Bowie. Each of these musicians approached the acoustic guitar in unique ways, from alternate tunings to percussive strumming and delicate fingerpicking. As you've seen, by now acoustic guitars were no longer just a background instrument but an integral part of rock's evolving sound.

To build on what you've learned, try exploring more altered tunings like DADGAD or Double Drop D, experiment with syncopated rhythms, or incorporate percussive strumming into your playing. If you've been working through the examples, consider transposing them to different keys or combining techniques from different artists to develop your own voice.

Chapter Five – Artists of the 1970s Part Two

In this chapter we'll continue our journey through the '70s, focusing on the artists who took acoustic playing in new directions. From the rich harmonies of The Eagles to the fingerpicking mastery of Lindsey Buckingham, you'll learn how the acoustic guitar became an integral part of rock's golden era.

The Eagles

Powerhouse country rock group The Eagles regularly placed acoustic guitars at the forefront of their music. From early tracks like *Take It Easy*, with its strummed acoustic foundation, to the legendary *Hotel California*, which was built around Don Felder's mysterious twelve-string intro, the acoustic guitar was an essential part of their sound. The band featured several guitarists, each with a different approach to acoustic playing: Don Felder, Glenn Frey, and Joe Walsh.

There are plenty of chord changes in this first example, but the slow, ballad feel makes it less challenging than it appears. Glenn Frey often used accompaniment parts like this one, which do not follow a simple I – IV – V sequence, but instead add movement and variation.

Example 5a

Joe Walsh takes the colour-chord concept a step further, moving away from open position. Notice how the open B string is used to add colour in bar four, turning a simple A Minor chord into the richer-sounding A Minor add 9. It is a simple trick, but it sounds fantastic on acoustic parts.

Example 5b

Pete Townshend was not the only guitarist to use triads against pedal tones and both Don Felder and Joe Walsh used this technique in The Eagles. Notice how you can move from a D Minor triad in bar one, through the G and F Major chords, and land on a D Major triad in bar two without it sounding jarring. Listen to *Bitter Creek* to hear a similar effect.

Example 5c

When you place your capo on the 7th fret, almost everything you play sounds a bit more like *Hotel California*! OK, that might be an exaggeration, but this register of the guitar sounds fantastic, and the capo lowers the action to make hammer-on and pull-offs easier to play. With the capo on, you will be playing Bm7 – Asus2 – Em7 – F#11.

Example 5d

Many of The Eagles' electric riffs made their way onto acoustic guitar as well. This Drop D country-style idea could sound equally at home on a Telecaster through a cranked Deluxe amp. The challenge here is clarity. Ensure that the open strings ring clearly against the fretted notes by keeping your fretting-hand placement clean.

Example 5e

Jackson Browne

A contemporary and friend of The Eagles, Jackson Browne actually wrote their early hit *Take It Easy*. He is a fantastic songwriter, and the acoustic guitar is central to both his playing and writing. He has frequently performed solo over the years, and the acoustic is the perfect instrument for accompaniment. His challenging fingerpicking parts often feature an alternating bass with syncopated melody notes layered on top.

A simple D Major, C Major, G Major progression is given more character with embellishments within the D Major chord. The C Major receives a subtle modification, transforming it into a rich-sounding Csus2 chord, a staple of 1970s acoustic rock and country.

Example 5f

Moving between high and low registers creates powerful acoustic parts. This example begins with Pete Townshend-style triads against a pedal tone (the open D string) before shifting to open position, landing on a sweet-sounding A7sus4 chord. This would work well as an intro, where the A7sus4 can resolve to either A Major or D Major.

Example 5g

Jackson Browne's playing frequently features rich chords that stop you in your tracks. Check out the F Major 9 in bar two. Try fingering it by hooking the thumb over the neck to fret the E string at the 1st fret. The third and fourth fingers should hold down the 3rd fret of the A and D strings while the first finger plays the B string at the 1st fret. The open strings should ring clearly, as they provide much of the chord's character.

Example 5h

With alternating bassline picking, the bass notes are usually played as "1 & 2 & 3 & 4 &." It is best to practice the bass part on its own first. The F Major chord is best played using a similar fingering to the FMaj9 in the previous example with the thumb hooked over the E string, third finger on the D string, and first on the B string. The second finger hammers on from the open G string to the 2nd fret.

Example 5i

When learning more complex parts, isolate the bass notes first. In this next example, the thumb alternates between the low D and regular D strings. When adding the melody, look for repeating rhythmic patterns. Bars one and two share the same rhythm, which then repeats in bar four.

Example 5j

Lindsey Buckingham

Fleetwood Mac went through various lineup changes over the years, but the arrival of Lindsey Buckingham introduced a seriously skilled musician on both electric and acoustic guitars. His Travis-picking style means you will hear many thumb-picked alternating basslines, often featuring difficult syncopated lines on top. To hear this in action, listen to his live solo version of *Big Love*, which sounds like two separate instruments being played at once.

Palm muting is common on electric guitar, but it adds power to acoustic playing as well, creating a chunky, percussive sound. This example features simple power chords, but the added palm muting makes them feel much bigger. Pay close attention to your palm placement and ensure you rest the flesh lightly on the saddle for the best effect.

Example 5k

Triads are an important musical device for guitarists, as they allow you to play in the mid-register while keeping a low string ringing underneath. This example, inspired by *Sara*, features the I chord moving to the II Major chord, (A Major to B Major). The pedal tones on the A string and open E string add colour and depth.

Example 5l

This time, the triads move from chord I to chord V (E Major). Playing triads in a higher register avoids the low-end muddiness that can sometimes build up when many musicians play in that open-position range. The arpeggiated picking patterns in bars two and four introduce an almost ragtime feel. Listen to *Never Going Back Again* for a similar effect.

Example 5m

Buckingham did not always use alternating basslines and instead sometimes played a steady stream of 1/8th note pulses on a single string with a syncopated melody on top. This example is played at a fast tempo, so begin slowly and only increase in speed once the melody feels natural. When it becomes comfortable, try palm-muting the bass notes. Check out *Big Love* for a similar approach.

Example 5n

Buckingham's blues fingerpicking is evident on tracks like *The Chain*. Drop the low E string down to D to perform the slow 1/4 note pulse The syncopated melody is based around an open D Major.

Example 5o

Tom Petty

From his work with The Heartbreakers to solo albums like Wildflowers, Tom Petty was a master of the acoustic guitar and used it for much more than simple strumming. As with Lindsey Buckingham, his playing featured rich (and sometimes unexpected) chord voicings, deft fingerpicking, and powerful Drop D ideas.

Many of us would play D Major to C Major using basic open chords, but Petty adds movement and tension here by incorporating ambiguous D suspended chords before passing through a b5 (Gb) to create tension on the C Major. Listen to *The Wild One* to hear this effect.

Example 5p

Petty's style often involves moving rapidly between chord shapes – an approach that's sometimes best played higher up the neck with a capo to avoid low end muddiness. The 5th fret capo also makes the part easier to play.

Example 5q

Capo Fret 5

Suspended chords can add softness and ambiguity to a progression. This example is in A Major, but the IV (D) and V (E) chords are played as sus2 and sus4 shapes instead of major chords.

Example 5r

Here's is a great voicing for an F#7 that's often used in rock and Americana. The open E string adds the 7th at the top, adding brightness to what could otherwise be a muddy-sounding barre chord. Hook the thumb over the 2nd fret of the E string, then use the third, second, and first fingers on the D, G, and B strings.

Example 5s

This Drop D arpeggiated riff creates a rich sound that's ideal for adding texture to acoustic rock. Though the chord movement is written out, most artists think of ideas like this as riffs rather than strict chord changes. Check out *Something Big* for a similar approach.

Example 5t

Boston

From the late 1970s to the early 1980s, a new radio-friendly commercial rock sound emerged that became known as adult-oriented rock (AOR). This softer rock style provided the perfect space for acoustic guitars to set up a track with an intro and verse before giving way to heavier guitar parts. Acoustic guitar truly found its home in the power ballads of this era.

Boston's Tom Scholz created a huge, layered acoustic sound by stacking both six- and twelve-string guitars in his recordings. The arpeggiated intro to their biggest hit, *More Than a Feeling* is a textbook example of simplicity and melody. This example explores how an open D Major chord can be used to create melodic ideas with minimal movement.

Example 5u

Scholz also brought a heavier, more electric-style attack to his acoustic playing. Here, his muted strings create a percussive, driving tone. To achieve this effect, release the pressure on the fretting fingers without lifting them off the strings, keeping the chord shape intact while striking the muted strings.

Example 5v

Heart

Heart's Nancy Wilson is a technically accomplished acoustic player, and some of her parts can be quite challenging. For some rock musicians, the acoustic guitar is simply a studio tool that can be used to add texture to a track. But this style of part writing shows that Wilson is clearly an accomplished acoustic guitarist, as comfortable there as she is on electric.

Wilson's driving rhythm style is a great strumming-hand workout, with flamenco-like energy. Spend time perfecting the suggested strumming pattern below, paying close attention to the tricky chord change to D Minor on the "&" of beat 4. Also note the D Minor/A chord, which lands on the "&" of beat 1 in bar two.

Example 5w

Heart's *Crazy on You* features an outrageous opening acoustic break, just like this next example. You can fingerpick this throughout, but the licks are easier to play with a pick, (although hybrid picking is another option). Use the pick for the D string while picking the B string with the middle finger.

Example 5x

Kansas

Kansas guitarist Kerry Livgren came from a jazz and classical background, but his progressive rock and psychedelic influences helped shape the band's sound. One of their biggest hits, *Dust in the Wind*, features a famous fingerpicked acoustic figure that Livgren originally wrote as a fingerpicking exercise.

The following example demonstrates how an alternating bassline and moving melody notes on open-position chords can quickly create a melodic, flowing part.

Example 5y

Moving inner voices while the outer voices remain in place adds a bit of drama and colour. In this example, the open A and B strings ring throughout while two-note intervals move between them. This simple technique adds movement and emotion and is often more expressive than simply sitting on an A Minor chord. If fingerpicking, use the thumb for the A and D strings, the index for the G string, and the middle for the B string.

Example 5z

We've now examined the rich harmonies and layered textures of The Eagles, the fluid fingerpicking of Lindsey Buckingham, and the intricate arrangements of Kansas and Heart. In the 1970s, acoustic guitar was no longer limited to being just an accompaniment – it was driving songs, shaping melodies, and adding depth to rock's biggest anthems.

To take your playing further, try layering multiple guitar parts, experiment with the open tunings used by artists like Tom Petty and Jackson Browne, or work on refining your strumming dynamics to capture the expressive range heard in this era. Pay close attention to how these musicians used acoustic textures in both soft ballads and high-energy rock songs.

As we move into the 1980s, we will see how the acoustic guitar adapted to a changing musical landscape. From the heartland rock of Bruce Springsteen to the refined fingerpicking of Mark Knopfler, acoustic guitar remained a vital part of rock music, even as production styles evolved. We'll also look at how it became a defining feature of the era's biggest power ballads, proving that the instrument could hold its own in an era of stadium rock.

Chapter Six – Artists of the 1980s

The sound of rock changed dramatically in first half of the 1980s as adult-oriented rock came to dominate the airwaves. Acoustic guitar parts became more dramatic, often occupying a main role in the intro and verses before giving way to heavily distorted guitar parts. Listen to Bon Jovi's *Wanted Dead or Alive* and you will hear this arrangement used to great effect.

Alongside this were Bruce Springsteen's Americana sound and Mark Knopfler's folk-inspired picking, which makes the '80s a decade full of varied acoustic guitar parts to explore. We will start with these two artists before exploring the commercial pop rock of acts like Bon Jovi.

Bruce Springsteen

Springsteen's reverence for the traditional American folk sound would later become one of the foundations of the Americana movement. His acoustic style is shaped by folk pioneers Woody Guthrie and Pete Seeger, and contrasts with the electric sound of the E Street Band. It has a wonderful intimacy and features driving rhythms with imaginative chord voicings.

A subtle but useful device in his playing is the use of a common tone between each chord. In this case, it is the G played at the 3rd fret of the high E string. Keep your fourth finger fretted here throughout to provide a strong, consistent sound as you move between chords.

Example 6a

Simple bass runs between chord changes showcase the folk and Americana elements of Springsteen's style in this example. In bar one, use your third finger on the D string, then play the run up the low E string with your first and second fingers, aiming to form the G5 chord shape when your second finger lands on the 3rd fret. Listen to *The River* to get a feel for this.

Example 6b

Springsteen is a solid fingerpicker, and this example shows his ability to use the technique in more challenging time signatures. We are in 6/8, so in bars two and three, count "1 2 & 3 & 4 5 6." When fingerpicking these bars, use the thumb and middle finger on beat 1, then alternate the thumb and your index on the D and G strings for the "2 & 3 &" counts.

Example 6c

Artists often have favourite rhythms and picking patterns that they use across different songs. Here, the rhythms and picking patterns from the previous example return, but are now applied to a different chord progression: F Major to C Major.

Example 6d

Fmaj   Cmaj

```
T---1----------------------------------------||---1----------------------------------||
A------------2-------2-------2-----||-----------0------0----------------||
B-------3-------3-------3-------3--||-3------2-----2------2----0----2--||
    ---1----------------------------------------||-------------------------------------------||
```

Springsteen is a master of Drop D tuning, using rich-sounding chords even in simple I – IV – V progressions. This example features a common D at the 3rd fret, which helps tie the changes together.

In bar one, place your third finger on the D string and your second on the B string. In bar two, keep the second finger in place while releasing the third, then use your first finger to play the 2nd fret. To play the A7sus4, move your first finger to the D string while keeping the second anchored on the B string.

Example 6e

Dmajadd4   Gmaj/B

```
E|------------------------------------------------------||--------------------------------------------------||
B|-----------------3--------------------3--||-----------------3---------------------3--||
G|----0-------0-----0------0-----0-----0--||----0-----0-----0------0-----0----0--||
D|--------4-------4---------4-------4------||----------0-------0---------0-------0----||
A|-------------------------------------------------------||-2--------------------2---------------------------||
D|-0-----------------------0-------------------------||----------------------------------------------------||
```

3
A7sus4   Dmajadd4

```
T|-----------------3--------------------3--||-----------------3---------------------3--||
A|----0-------0-----0------0-----0-----0--||----0-----0-----0------0-----0----0--||
  |--------2-------2---------2-------2------||----------4-------4---------4-------4----||
B|-0-----------------------0-------------------------||-0----------------------0---------------------------||
```

Mark Knopfler

Mark Knopfler's playing spans a huge range of styles and approaches on both electric and acoustic guitar. His acoustic approach blends folk fingerpicking, blues picking, and ragtime, all played with superb timing, tone, and precision. Acoustic guitar and resonator have always been central to his work, from Dire Straits tracks like *Romeo and Juliet* to his comprehensive catalogue of solo albums.

This example shows how to create interesting accompaniment parts using sus chords instead of remaining on the I Major chord. Use your second finger on the D string, third on the G string, and fourth on the B string. This position creates room to move the fourth finger up a fret to play the Asus4 chord in bar two.

Example 6f

These colour chords are similar to those found in Knopfler's *Sailing to Philadelphia*. The underlying F# Minor to A Major (vi – I) progression is simple, but by using open strings on the F# and playing from the 5th (C#) instead of the root, the vi chord obtains a more complex sound. Use your third finger on the A string and your fourth on the D string and ensure the open strings ring cleanly.

Example 6g

Knopfler regularly creates a percussive attack by using just his thumb and index finger in a pick-like position. In this example, use the thumb to pluck the open D string, then flick downward with the nail of the index finger to play the G, B, and D strings. Repeat the same movement in bar two, but with the thumb playing the A string and the index flicking the D, G, and B strings.

Example 6h

Here's another *Sailing to Philadelphia*-style part featuring interesting voicings for E Major and A Major. Instead of open position chords, Knopfler uses mid-register triads. The first inversion A Major, with the 3rd (C#) in the bass, creates a smooth transition into the root-position D Major.

Example 6i

The decorated A Minor chord in bar one includes a classic 1960s folk-style move with a pull-off on the B string. Finger the A Minor chord as normal, then play the pull-off on beat 2 with your fourth finger at the 3rd fret.

Example 6j

[musical notation — Example 6j, chords: Am, Gmaj, Gsus4, G6/9]

Richie Sambora

Bon Jovi were one of the biggest bands of the '80s, and Richie Sambora wrote some their most memorable acoustic riffs. *Wanted Dead or Alive* has been essential learning for guitarists since its release in 1986. Sambora's writing flows effortlessly from acoustic parts into heavy electric riffs.

These palm-muted chords echo Lindsey Buckingham, producing a similarly chunky sound. The part is based around a common tone: the F# at the 4th fret of the D string. Keep your fourth finger fretted here throughout and listen to the colour this note adds to each chord. Use downstrokes throughout for an even tone.

Example 6k

[musical notation — Example 6k, bar 1: chords B5, A6, with P.M.]

[musical notation — Example 6k, bar 3: chords GMaj7, GMaj7, Esus2, with P.M.]

Most guitarists have their own variation of the D Major, Dsus2, and Dsus4 chord patterns that are usually created by the rhythm they choose to play. In a similar way, instead of simply playing A Major and C Major, this example moves between A7sus4 and Cadd9 for smoother chord transitions. The common tones on the B and E strings remain consistent between both chords.

Example 6l

Wanted Dead or Alive features a brilliant cascading open phrase played against an open D pedal tone. You can replicate this effect by moving down the B and E strings playing the D Minor scale in 3rds. It is an evocative sound, and once you've learned the idea, try reversing it to ascend the neck.

Example 6m

Sambora gets great mileage out of a single chord by moving notes within the shape. Start with your third finger on the low E string and your fourth on the B string. Next, move your first finger to the B string, before finally placing your second on the G string to complete the Gadd9 chord.

Example 6n

Common tones and moving basslines are central to this part. Use your third and fourth fingers on the B and E strings while your first and second fingers handle the bass notes on the A string. Many guitarists struggle with an open-position G Minor chord, so use this Gm/Bb shape as your go-to open position G Minor voicing.

Example 6o

In this chapter we've explored some of the diverse acoustic styles that shaped rock music in the 1980s. From the folk-inspired fingerpicking of Mark Knopfler to the power ballads of Richie Sambora, this decade showed how acoustic guitar remained an essential part of rock's evolution. You have seen how artists blended strumming, intricate picking patterns, and creative chord voicings to craft memorable parts that stood out in both electric and acoustic-driven songs.

To build on these techniques, try combining percussive strumming with hybrid picking or experiment with Drop D tuning to create deeper, fuller sounds. Pay close attention to the way players like Bruce Springsteen and Mark Knopfler use dynamics to shape their performances. Their ability to shift between soft, delicate passages and powerful, driving rhythms is what gives their acoustic playing so much character.

As we move on, we will explore how the acoustic guitar evolved through the 1990s and beyond. A new generation of players emerged, drawing inspiration from classic rock while adding their own modern twists. From the raw, emotive playing of John Frusciante to the anthemic, acoustic-driven songs of Noel Gallagher, these artists pushed the instrument in fresh directions.

Chapter Seven – Artists of the 1990s and Beyond

In the 1990s, a new generation of artists emerged who took the influences of previous decades and shaped them in original ways. Alternative bands like R.E.M. wove acoustic-driven tracks into their sound, blending jangly, folk-inspired playing with modern rock energy. Guitarists like Rich Robinson of The Black Crowes embraced a retro style, channelling the raw swagger of Keith Richards and the intricate layering of Jimmy Page. His Open G tuning work, particularly on songs like *She Talks to Angels*, helped revive classic rock techniques for a new audience.

Meanwhile, in the UK, Britpop exploded, with bands like Oasis and their chief songwriter, Noel Gallagher, proving that the acoustic guitar could drive anthems just as powerfully as electric guitars. Gallagher's use of colourful chord voicings and propulsive strumming defined a generation of singalong classics, with *Wonderwall* becoming one of the most instantly recognisable acoustic riffs of all time.

The decade also saw an increasing use of the acoustic guitar as a central instrument in alternative rock. John Frusciante of the Red Hot Chili Peppers infused funk and flamenco elements into his acoustic playing, creating dynamic and percussive textures that gave songs like *Breaking the Girl* a distinctive feel. Grunge and post-grunge acts such as Pearl Jam brought an introspective, storytelling quality to their acoustic work, particularly in their MTV Unplugged performances. Artists across the spectrum experimented with fingerpicking, unusual tunings, and percussive techniques, proving that the acoustic guitar remained as vital to rock as ever.

John Frusciante

The Red Hot Chili Peppers' early funk sound was driven by Frusciante's Hendrix-inspired Stratocaster riffs and rhythms. The band changed guitarists multiple times through the 1980s, but when Frusciante returned for the Blood Sugar Sex Magik album, he brought a new acoustic presence with him. His parts can be challenging and feature tricky syncopations over alternating basslines.

We'll start with a cool yet accessible idea that is both powerful and creative. The idea is to move the easy open E Major shape up the neck in a 6/8 rhythm, so count "1 2& 3& 4 5 6." Try adding a capo at the 2nd fret or higher to brighten the sound and remove some low-end mud. Listen to Frusciante's acoustic part on *Breaking the Girl* for a similar effect.

Example 7a

Acoustic guitars do not always have to be strummed and can sound incredibly effective for simple riffs like the one below. If you are fingerpicking, use the thumb and index finger throughout. In bar one, the thumb plays the notes on the A string while the index finger plucks the D string. In the second half of bar two, the thumb plays the E string while the index finger sounds the D string.

You can also play this with a pick, using alternate picking in bar one and hybrid picking in bar two. This means using the pick for the E string while simultaneously plucking the D string with the middle finger. The open D string can be played with either the pick or the middle finger, depending on what feels most natural.

Example 7b

A pulsating bassline on the D and A strings drives this next example, but the challenge lies in the speed at which Frusciante plays it. You will hear a similar approach on the Chili Peppers' *Road Trippin'*, where the bassline maintains a steady pulse while the melody adds movement on top.

At this tempo, it is best to play the B string with the index finger and the E string with the middle. The more traditional approach of using the middle and ring finger can be harder to articulate cleanly.

Example 7c

Frusciante's acoustic playing often carries a strong Spanish, Mexican or flamenco influence, blending percussive attack with rapid melodic runs. While a flamenco player would typically perform this fingerstyle, using a pick here will help maintain accuracy and attack.

In bar one, when you play the final 1/16th note of beat 2, use an upstroke with the pick. This will allow you to start beat 3 with a downstroke, setting up a clean alternate picking pattern for each 1/6th note. The same approach should be used in bar two when you reach the final 1/16th of the beat on the open B string. Keeping this picking pattern consistent will ensure smooth, fluid phrasing.

Example 7d

This next example also features a pulsating bassline, but there are two key aspects to focus on. First, listen to my recording for how the swing feel should sound. Second, the thumb picks the bassline on beat 1, sustaining over beat 2 before being plucked again on beats 3 and 4. This requires more focus than the typical 1 2 3 4 bassline approach.

Example 7e

Noel Gallagher

Noel Gallagher is an interesting artist. He is not especially technical, but his acoustic playing features great use of chord tones and colour chords, along with distinctive rhythm playing. And everybody will ask you to play *Wonderwall*!

Let's start with Noel's preferred chord voicings, which he has used frequently throughout his career. The first chord in each bar is a standard major or minor shape, followed by the version that Noel generally uses instead.

Example 7f

Next, here is a typical Noel rhythm part with the *Wonderwall* vibe. Like the chords, this is a pattern he has used and varied slightly on many tracks over the years. Part of the magic comes from pushing the chord on beat 3 by a 1/16th note. Try my suggested strumming pattern here.

Example 7g

Adding some colourful chords to that rhythm creates a strong musical part. Listen to Noel's work with Oasis and in his solo career, and you will discover that rhythms like these are the foundation of his playing.

Example 7h

Noel also uses the technique of moving chords up against open strings to great effect. In this example, a simple I – II – V chord progression of E Major, F# Major, and B Major becomes far more interesting.

Example 7i

Noel does use other rhythms too! This example uses common tones at the 3rd fret of the B and E strings, so the third and fourth fingers stay in place throughout. To play the D chord, hook the thumb over to fret the 2nd fret of the low E string.

Example 7j

Pearl Jam

One of the most interesting acoustic aspects of the 1990s was the arrival of the MTV Unplugged series, which saw artists of all genres rework their electric pieces for acoustic guitar. It is fascinating to see grunge bands like Alice in Chains and Nirvana strip back their heavier tracks. Pearl Jam, one of the biggest grunge bands, increasingly featured acoustic parts in their output over the years.

Here is a great example of how more interesting chord choices make a progression come alive. Underlying it all is a simple C Major, A Minor, and E Minor progression, but the Maj7 and sus chords add personality.

Example 7k

It's common to hear the echoes of previous generations in any artist's music, and this fingerpicked part, inspired by Pearl Jam's *Just Breathe*, has a strong Kansas *Dust in the Wind* vibe.

Example 7l

Breaking up chords with licks and fills adds variety to any part. Here, we add interest with a 1/4 note triplet figure in bar two that creates a great transition from D to G.

Example 7m

Peter Buck

Some artists feature acoustic guitars frequently, while for others, it plays an important but supporting role. Then, there are players like R.E.M.'s Peter Buck, who have complete control over the acoustic guitar and introduce other folk instruments like mandolins and bouzoukis.

Moving simple chord shapes up and down the neck while playing them against open strings can create surprising effects. The Dadd11 in bar three is just an open-position C Major shape moved up two frets. Here, the open G string adds the colour of a 4th, and the open E string adds a 9th.

Try moving other open chord shapes around and listen for the effect of the open strings against them. Check out R.E.M.'s *Man on the Moon* to hear this in action.

Example 7n

Sometimes, playing in a different time signature breathes new life into well-worn chord progressions. In this example, a I – ii – bVII – IV chord progression gains a fresh feel in 6/8. Count the "1 2& 3& 4 5& 6&" rhythm.

Example 7o

Another simple chord progression gains character by adding open strings for more colour. In this A Major to Bm sequence, the Bm11 chord in bar two makes it sound much more interesting.

Example 7p

This example demonstrates how syncopated rhythms can enhance simple chord sequences. The challenge lies in playing on the offbeats, particularly coming in on the "&" of beat 1 in bars two and four.

Example 7q

Here is a simple yet gorgeous example influenced by R.E.M.'s *Sweetness Follows*. Many songwriters would sit on a basic D Major chord, but Buck always searches for colour and interest. Drop the low E string to D and see how much depth the open strings can add when played against a few choice fretted notes.

Example 7r

Dmaj9   D6/9sus4

```
    E—0———0———0———0———0———0———0———0——|—0———0———0———0———0———0———0———0—
T   B—2———2———2———2———2———2———2———2——|—0———0———0———0———0———0———0———0—
A   G—2———2———2———2———2———2———2———2——|—0———0———0———0———0———0———0———0—
B   D—0———0———0———0———0———0———0———0——|—0———0———0———0———0———0———0———0—
    A—0———0———0———0———0———0———0———0——|—0———0———0———0———0———0———0———0—
    D—0———0———0———0———0———0———0———0——|—0———0———0———0———0———0———0———0—
```

Rich Robinson

The Black Crowes' retro, rootsy sound is both familiar and unique. There's an obvious Rolling Stones influence, but the band developed their own voice, particularly on tracks like *She Talks to Angels*. Brothers Chris and Rich Robinson had a perfect synergy between voice and guitar, and Rich's Keith Richards-inspired parts are essential learning, especially if you are exploring Open G tuning.

Start by tuning to Open G Major which, low to high, is:

D, G, D, G, B, D.

Now place a capo at the 4th fret, as altered tunings in the open position can sound a bit too full and muddy.

Begin with the Keith Richards-style hammer-on to the D and B strings using the second and first fingers, respectively. Use plenty of force so the open strings don't overshadow these notes.

Example 7s

Capo Fret 4

Gmaj   Cmaj/E   Csus2   Gmaj

```
    D—0—————————0—————————0————————|—5———5———5———5———X———X———0—
T   B—0⌣—1——————1—————————————1————|—3———3———3———3———X———X———0—
A   G—0———⌣—————0—————————————————0|—0———0———0———0———X———X———0—
B   D—0————2————2—————————————————— |—0———0———0———0———X———X———0—
    G—0————————————————————————————|—5———5———5———5———X———X———0—
    D——————————————————————————————|——————————————————————————
```

Now, move the capo to the 3rd fret for this example inspired by the band's track *Non-Fiction*. Robinson's playing is filled with cool licks, and to play the fill in bar two, use the first finger at the 2nd fret, then slide on the A string with the second before finishing with a second-to-third finger hammer-on.

Example 7t

Capo Fret 3

G7sus4/D   Gmaj/D

```
D-3----3--3--3--3------0--------|--------------------------------------|
B-1----1--1--1--1------0--------|--------------------------------------|
G-0----0--0--0--0------0--------|------------0-------------------------0|
D-0----0--0--0--0------0--------|--2-----------------0------------------|
G-------------------------------|----3/4----------------0----4--5-------|
D-------------------------------|--------------------------------------|
```

When playing in open tunings, conventional chord fingerings go out the window, which can lead to some interesting new shapes. At the end of bar two, form the G7 by placing the second finger on the D string and the third and fourth fingers on the B and E strings. Keep these in place, then add the first on the A string for the A11#5.

Example 7u

G5   Cmadd9/G   G7no3rd

```
D-5----5--5--5--5--5------0--------|--0----0--0--0--0------3|
B-3----3--3--3--3--3------1--------|--1----1--1--1--1------3|
G-0----0--0--0--0--0------0--------|--0----0--0--0--0------0|
D-0----0--0--0--0--0------1--------|--1----1--1--1--1------3|
G-0----0--0--0--0--0------0--------|--0----0--0--0--0------0|
D----------------------------------|-----------------------|
```

G7no3rd   **A11♯5**

In bar two of the next example, use an index finger barre for the chords at the 3rd and 5th frets, releasing pressure to play muted chords on beats 2 and 3 while keeping the open A string ringing. You can hear this type of percussive playing on *Thorn in My Pride*.

Example 7v

Capo Fret 4

G6   **Gmaj**   **Gm7**   **Cmaj/G**   **Gm7**   **Cadd9/G**   **Gmaj**

This example is inspired by Robinson's gorgeous opening lick on *She Talks to Angels*. While the opening phrase looks daunting, most of the work comes from the picking hand. In the fretting hand, try using the second or third finger on the G string and the first for the hammer-on/pull-offs on the D string.

Example 7w

Slash/Izzy Stradlin'

Guns N' Roses practically defined the hard rock sound that evolved at the end of the 1980s. Reacting against the glossy hair metal of the decade, they arrived with bone-crunching riffs and raw production. Yet, they also produced rootsy acoustic tracks and fantastic ballads on their *Patience* EP and later on the two *Use Your Illusion* albums.

There's a clear Keith Richards influence in both Slash and Izzy's acoustic playing, usually in their approaches to playing embellished chords. The main challenge here is keeping the fretted fingers stable while the others play the hammer-ons and pull-offs.

Example 7x

These *Patience*-inspired licks demonstrate how he might solo over the previous chord. String bending on acoustic is tricky, and most players opt for a semitone bend rather than a full tone. Use the third finger to bend and reinforce it with one or two fingers for extra strength.

Example 7y

Cmaj Gmaj

Dmaj Amaj

This *One in a Million*-style chord progression features rapid changes. Notice how the third finger stays on the 3rd fret and acts as an anchor while the others move.

Example 7z

Dmaj Dsus2sus4 Cadd9 Gmaj

Playing alternate voicings in basic chord movements can make progressions sound far more sophisticated. The D Major/F# is a great alternative to a standard open D Major shape, with the F# in the bass moving smoothly to G Major.

Example 7z1

Sheryl Crow

Sheryl Crow rose to prominence with her 1994 album *Tuesday Night Music Club*, which produced the smash hit *All I Wanna Do*. However, she had already spent years in the music industry as an established jingle writer and backing vocalist on Michael Jackson's "Bad" world tour. She is a great study, and her playing suggests she writes primarily on acoustic rather than using it simply as a layering tool.

Playing in 3/4 can be trickier than it seems, and if you are new to the time signature, you may find yourself searching for beat 4. Given the level of detail in this example, start very slowly with a "1 e & a 2 e & a 3 e & a" count throughout. Check out Crow's *Strong Enough* to hear her play in 3/4.

Example 7z2

To create the choppy effect in this next example, use your picking hand palm to mute the strings at the start of beat 4. Pick through the chord on beat 2, mute the notes with your palm, then come back in on the "&" of beat 4.

Example 7z3

This chord/lick writing technique can make acoustic parts much more interesting. Use your third finger to play the slide and pull-off lick on beat 2, ensuring that the pull-off from the 2nd fret to the open string is strong. You will hear similar ideas in her track, *C'mon C'mon*.

Example 7z4

At various points in this book, you have seen how useful the D Major/F# chord can be. In bar two, you will find this voicing moved two frets higher to form an E/G#. Use the third finger on the low E string, the first finger on the D string, and the fourth finger on the G string.

Example 7z5

When Crow plays unplugged versions of her electric tracks, replicating the original acoustic parts can be a challenge, so practicing barre chords on acoustic, along with their embellishments, builds strength and control. Use a first-finger barre at the 5th fret, placing the third finger on the 7th fret of the A string and the fourth on the 7th fret of the G string. Watch out for the pull-off from the 7th to 5th fret in bar one.

Example 7z6

Johnny Buckland/Chris Martin

Both Chris Martin and Johnny Buckland contribute acoustic guitar parts to Coldplay's tracks, and it was vocalist Martin who played the distinctive acoustic rhythm part on the band's breakthrough hit *Yellow*. Some artists use common alternate tunings like DADGAD, but in Buckland and Martin's playing, you will find more unusual tunings, akin to Nick Drake's style.

Tuning the high E string down to C# is a simple altered tuning that yields great musical results. To play the F#m11, hook your thumb over the neck to fret the 2nd fret of the E string. Use the third and fourth fingers on the A and D strings and the first finger on the G string.

Example 7z7

TUNING LOW TO HIGH - EADGBC#

The same tuning is used to add life to a simple E Minor to A Major chord sequence. Altered tunings like this allow you to create interesting chords like Em6 with minimal effort and leave your other fingers free to add decoration and colour.

Example 7z8

TUNING LOW TO HIGH - EADGBC#

Aadd9   **A5 A6/9 Aadd9**

```
3
T|--0----0---0---0---0---0-----0---0---0---0-----0----0----0----0----0----3-----1-----0---|
A|--0----0---0---0---0---0-----0---0---0---0-----0----0----0----0----0----0-----0-----0---|
B|--2----2---2---2---2---2-----2---2---2---2-----2----2----2----2----2----2-----2-----2---|
 |--2----2---2---2---2---2-----2---2---2---2-----2----2----2----2----2----2-----2-----2---|
 |--0----0---0---0---0---0-----0---0---0---0-----0----0----0----0----0----0-----0-----0---|
```

Retune to Open G Major (D G D G B D) for this final example. While this tuning appeared earlier in the Rich Robinson section, the approach here is quite different. Altered tunings often unlock new ideas, and in this example, moving the same shape up and down the neck creates a fresh twist.

Example 7z9

TUNING LOW TO HIGH - DGDGBD

E♭maj7   **B♭6/9**   **C(add9)**

```
 D|--0----0------0---0---0---0-----0----0---0---0---0---0---0---0----0----0----0---0---0---0---0---0--|
 B|--6----6------6---6---6---6-----1----1---1---1---1---1---1---1----5----5----5---5---5---5---5---5--|
 G|--0----0------0---0---0---0-----0----0---0---0---0---0---0---0----0----0----0---0---0---0---0---0--|
 D|--8----8------8---8---8---8-----3----3---3---3---3---3---3---3----5----5----5---5---5---5---5---5--|
 G|--8----8------8---8---8---8-----3----3---3---3---3---3---3---3----5----5----5---5---5---5---5---5--|
 D|----------------------------------------------------------------------------------------------------|
```

We've seen how acoustic guitar evolved in the 1990s, with artists blending past influences into fresh, innovative styles. From John Frusciante's intricate rhythmic phrasing to Noel Gallagher's bold, anthemic strumming, each player brought something unique to the instrument. The acoustic guitar remained a defining voice in rock, whether in stripped-down MTV Unplugged performances or stadium-filling singalongs.

Now that you have explored a wide range of techniques and styles, it is time to put them all together. In the next two chapters, you will apply what you've learned by studying two complete pieces that combine different approaches into full-length musical performances. These will challenge your technique, timing, and dynamics, helping you develop a well-rounded and expressive acoustic style.

Let's dive in…

Chapter Eight – Study Track One

In this chapter, you will use the techniques and ideas studied throughout this book in a real-world musical situation. This track is inspired by the rootsy style of Keith Richards from The Rolling Stones. Acoustic guitar parts like this are designed to support vocals, and while the goal is not to overpower the mix, there is still plenty of room to use the colour chord approach studied earlier.

The track is built around an A Major to D Major chord progression, with the bVII G Major chord making an occasional appearance. Begin by familiarising yourself with the gentle swing rhythm by listening to the audio track. Keep your strumming hand relaxed and use a thinner pick to brighten the tone. Strumming directions have been included for each section, with bar one providing the pattern for the first five bars. The pattern in bar six continues in bars seven and eight.

Notice how the common I – IV progression is given more interest by the addition of suspended chords on both the A and D.

From bar ten, the focus shifts from the weighty, full-bodied sound of open position chords to simple three-note voicings on the G, B, and E strings. Moving away from the lower register can be useful, particularly if a piano is filling out the low end.

The chord in bar ten is a streamlined A Major voicing, best played using the second finger on the G string and the third finger on the B string. While a full A Major chord is tempting, limiting yourself to two fretted notes makes the hammer-on from the open B string to the second fret smoother. This fingering also allows for an effortless transition to the G6/B chord that follows. Simply shift the second finger to the G string and place the first finger on the B string.

In bar fifteen, the closing lick after the Dsus2/A can be played either with a pick or by hybrid picking. If the latter, the pick should strike the D string while the middle finger plucks the B.

Example 8a:

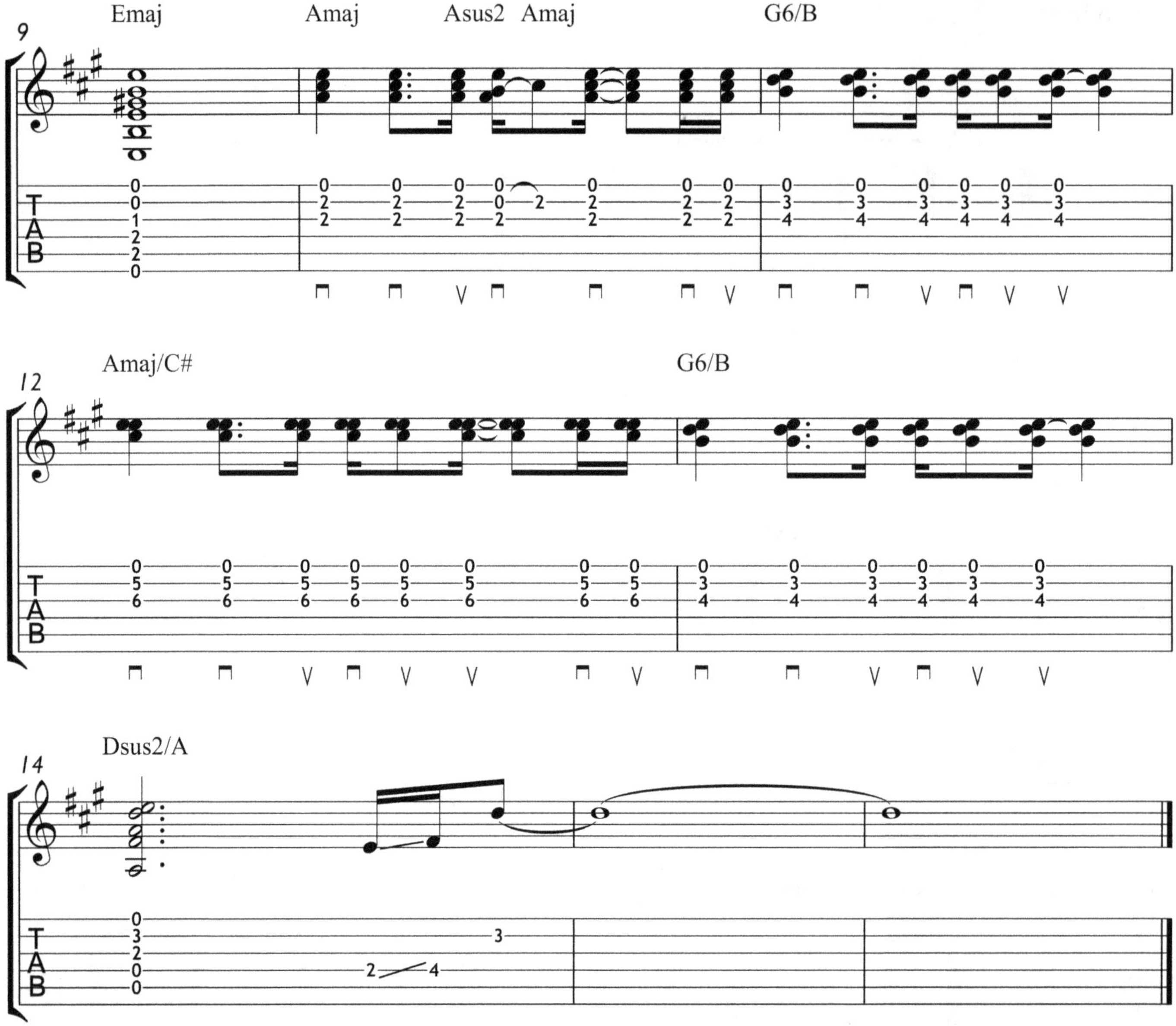
9
Emaj
Amaj
Asus2
Amaj
G6/B
12
Amaj/C#
G6/B
14
Dsus2/A
T
A
B

Chapter Nine – Study Track Two

This track is inspired by the acoustic rock style of The Who's Pete Townshend and features two distinct sections. The first showcases Townshend's ability to add colour in the open position, paired with his powerful, almost frenetic strumming style. The second half demonstrates his creative use of triads against pedal tones, with the open D string providing continuity.

Power chords are a hallmark of Townshend's style, even in open position. In bar one, you will play a G5 chord, which resembles an open G Major shape but omits the major 3rd (B). Finger this chord as you would an open G Major, but lightly rest your first finger against the A and D strings to keep them muted. The third and fourth fingers remain on the B and high E strings respectively. At the end of the bar, shift the first finger to high E string to form a G7(no 3rd) chord.

Bar three introduces another variation of G7(no 3rd). Keep the third and fourth fingers on the B and high E strings while positioning the second finger on the D string, then add the first finger at the 2nd fret. Townshend also favoured the softer sound of Maj7 chords so pay close attention to the FMaj7/C chord in bar five to appreciate the warmth and subtle complexity it adds.

The tone shifts in bar nine as triads are played against the open D string, creating an instantly recognisable Townshend texture. Writing acoustic parts in this manner keeps the arrangement clear, preventing muddiness in the low end while allowing space for electric guitar parts. The open D string acts as a pedal tone, smoothing transitions between the D Major and F Major chords, which might otherwise sound jarring if played in open position.

Common tones also play a crucial role in glueing the part together. In bar nine, the A note at the fifth fret of the high E string is present in both the D Major and F Major chords, creating a seamless shift. The triads on the G, B, and high E strings never move too drastically, ensuring smooth voice leading and keeping movement small so nothing clashes with a vocal melody.

These triads should not present major fingering challenges, but be mindful of how you approach the C Maj/G chord. Use a partial barre with the first finger at the 8th fret of the B and high E strings, while the second finger frets the 9th fret of the G string. The transitions between chords are quite rapid so take your time mastering them before building up speed gradually. It's important to maintain accuracy and pay close attention to the rhythm throughout.

Example 9a:

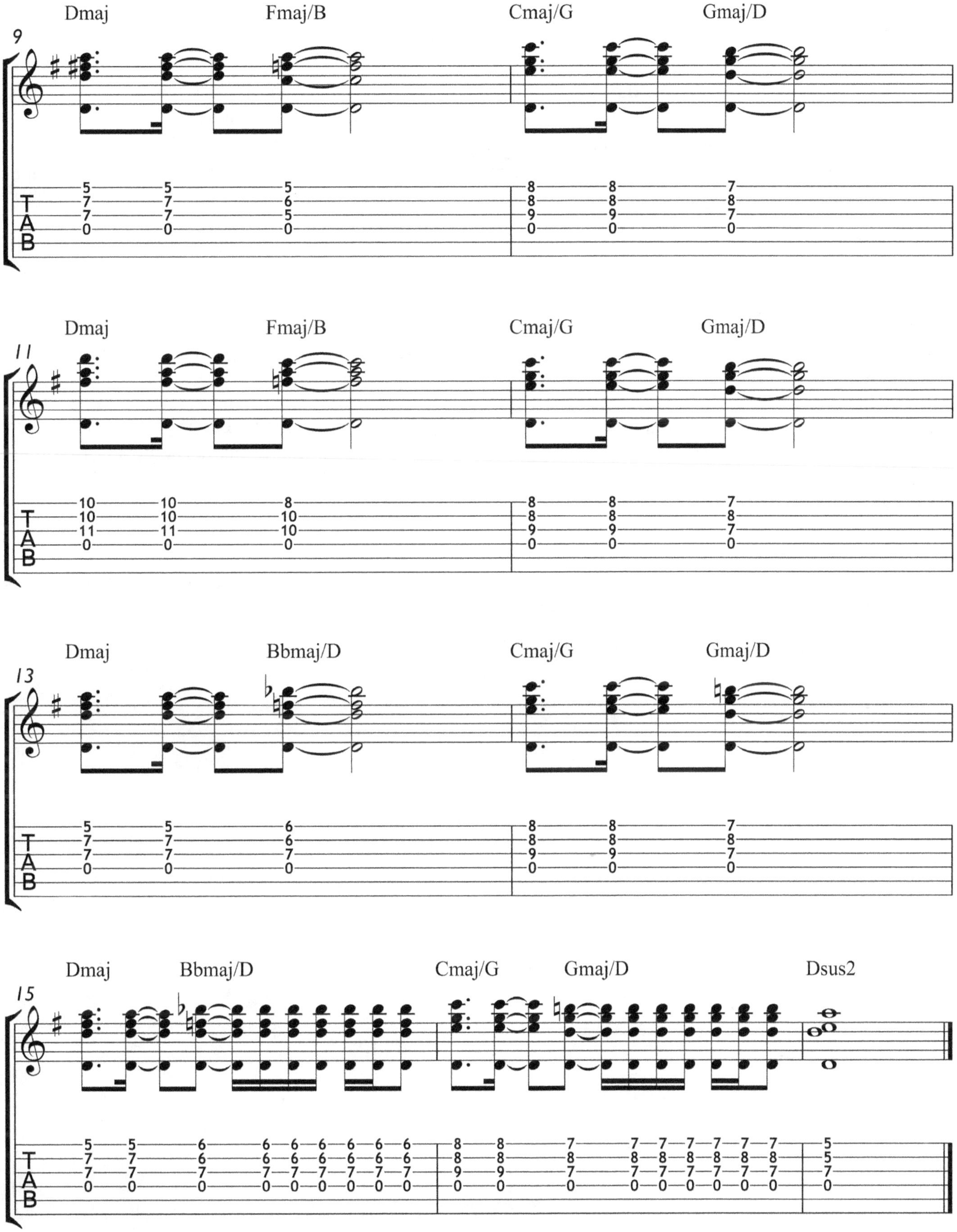
9
Dmaj
Fmaj/B
Cmaj/G
Gmaj/D
11
Dmaj
Fmaj/B
Cmaj/G
Gmaj/D
13
Dmaj
Bbmaj/D
Cmaj/G
Gmaj/D
15
Dmaj
Bbmaj/D
Cmaj/G
Gmaj/D
Dsus2

Conclusion

I hope you've enjoyed this journey through the development of acoustic guitar in rock music. Over the past sixty-five years, the instrument has evolved from a simple rhythm tool into a defining voice in countless iconic songs. Whether it is the delicate fingerpicking of Paul Simon, the driving strumming of Pete Townshend, or the inventive rhythms of John Frusciante, the acoustic guitar has proven to be as expressive and powerful as any other instrument in rock.

As you have worked through this book, you will have seen how acoustic players take influence from the past while forging their own styles. Many of the techniques covered here, such as colour chords, alternate tunings, and rhythmic embellishments, occur across many decades and genres and are constantly reinterpreted. Now that you have studied these examples, your next step is to apply them to your own playing. Experiment with moving chord shapes around the neck, try fingerpicking patterns on new progressions, or explore altered tunings to find fresh ideas.

There are countless artists beyond those featured in this book who are worth studying. If you love the bluesy acoustic work of Keith Richards and Jimmy Page, check out Ry Cooder and Richard Thompson. If you are drawn to the intricate fingerpicking of Mark Knopfler and Lindsey Buckingham, listen to Bert Jansch and Chet Atkins. If the songwriting styles of Bruce Springsteen and Noel Gallagher inspire you, dig into Tom Petty and Neil Young.

Most importantly, keep playing! The acoustic guitar is an instrument that rewards exploration, whether you are sitting alone writing a song or backing a full band.

Keep challenging yourself and enjoy the journey.

www.ingramcontent.com/pod-product-compliance
Lightning Source LLC
Chambersburg PA
CBHW081432090426
42740CB00017B/3281